2015 NACWE Prayer Call Handouts

2015 NACWE Prayer Call Handouts, Copyright 2017 by National Association of Christian Women Entrepreneurs (NACWE)

Scripture quotations marked (NIV) are taken from the Holy Bible, New International Version®, NIV®. Copyright © 1973, 1978, 1984, 2011 by Biblica, Inc.™ Used by permission of Zondervan. All rights reserved worldwide. www.zondervan.com. The "NIV" and "New International Version" are trademarks registered in the United States Patent and Trademark Office by Biblica, Inc.™

Scripture quotations marked (ESV) are from The ESV® Bible (The Holy Bible, English Standard Version®), copyright © 2001 by Crossway, a publishing ministry of Good News Publishers. Used by permission. All rights reserved.

All NACWE prayer call handouts were inserted in their original format, which accounts for various inconsistencies throughout the book.

RHEMA Publishing House
rhemapublishinghouse.com
PO Box 1244 McKinney, TX 75070

ISBN: 978-0-9990932-3-8

Welcome to the Soul of NACWE!

The National Association of Christian Women Entrepreneurs (NACWE) has always been known for its heart, and we want to formally introduce you to our prayer and devotion corner, the Soul of NACWE. Our sisterhood is here to support you on your personal journey of faith and how that is intertwined with your business. We believe in the transforming power of prayer.

- We pray daily for our Members
- We pray together weekly in a special Members call
- We hand out a weekly Prayer Call guide, and we offer these to you in this booklet.

In our businesses, God is our CEO.

For Members of the National Association of Christian Women Entrepreneurs, Devotion to God comes first and we are reminded of the acrostic: **J - O - Y**

J stands for Jesus—He comes first.
O stands for others—they come next.
Y stands for yourself—and in this group, your Entrepreneurial endeavors!

Jesus First: *"But seek first the kingdom of God and his righteousness, and all these things will be added to you."* Matthew 6:33

Others Next: *"As each has received a gift, use it to serve one another, as good stewards of God's varied grace..."* 1 Peter 4:10

Your Work: *"Commit your work to the Lord, and your plans will be established."* Proverbs 16:3

LEADERS AND MEMBERS IN NACWE ARE COMMITTED
AND DEDICATED TO GOD AND HIS WAYS.

Thank you to all who have led us in these endeavors by managing, leading, writing, and praying; you are SO dear to us!
 -Barbara Hollace, Sally Adamcik, Marian Struble, Diane Cunningham, Karen Lindwall-Bourg, and Courtenay Blackwell
  -and all participating NACWE Members

Prayer Calls 2015

Believe 1
Submit 2
Transformation 3
Healthy 4

Renew 5
Bold 6
Connect 7
Joy 8

Shine 9
Love 10
Trust 11
Humility 12
Sacrifice 13

Redeemed 14
Persistence 15
Compassion 16
Action 17

Encourage 18
Diligence 19
Desire 20
Grace 21

Passion 22
Prayer 23
Fear 24
Imagination 25
Victory 26

Sharpen 27
Abide 28
Compassion 29
Pride 30

Hope	31
Mercy	32
Empower	33
Covenant	34
Forgiveness	35
Prosper	36
Obedience	37
Restore	38
Peace	39
Comfort	40
Rigteousness	41
Truth	42
Stronghold	43
Praise	44
Fellowship	45
Thanksgiving	46
Purpose	47
Inspire	48
Celebrate	49

NACWE Word of the Week: Study and Discussion
The Word of the Week is: Believe

Definition- be·lieve

bəˈlēv/ (google) *verb*
1. accept (something) as true; feel sure of the truth of.

   synonyms: be convinced by, trust, have confidence in, consider honest, consider truthful

2. hold (something) as an opinion; think or suppose.

   synonyms: think, be of the opinion that, have an idea that, imagine, suspect, suppose, assume, presume, take it, conjecture, surmise, conclude, deduce, understand, be given to understand, gather, fancy, guess, dare say

Scripture

1. **Matthew 21:22 NIV /** If you believe, you will receive whatever you ask for in prayer."
2. **Mark 9:24 ESV /** Immediately the father of the child cried out and said, "I believe; help my unbelief!"
3. **Romans 4:3 ESV /** For what does the Scripture say? "Abraham believed God, and it was counted to him as righteousness."

Quote

"*Don't limit yourself. Many people limit themselves to what they think they can do. You can go as far as your mind lets you. What you believe, remember, you can achieve.*" ~~Mary Kay Ash

Questions

1. If you choose the word "Believe" for 2015, how would you hope to be changed by the study of the word? If you didn't choose it, how do you think a person might be changed by studying the word?

2. In the verse Mark 9:24, he talks about having belief and unbelief. Do you think you can have both at the same time? How and why?

3. What would you hope to gain, or change by studying one word for the year?

© 2015 National Association of Christian Women Entrepreneurs * All Rights Reserved * www.nacwe.org

NACWE Word of the Week: Study and Discussion
January 12th 2015

The Word of the Week is: Submit

Definition- Submit
[s*uh* b-**mit**]

Verb

1. to give over or yield to the power or authority of another.

2. to subject to some kind of treatment or influence.

Scripture

Hebrews 13:17
Have confidence in your leaders and **submit** to their authority, because they keep watch over you as those who must give an account. Do this so that their work will be a joy, not a burden, for that would be of no benefit to you.

James 4:7
Submit yourselves, then, to God. Resist the devil, and he will flee from you.

Quotation

"Submission is not about authority and it is not obedience; it is all about relationships of love and respect." — Wm. Paul Young, *The Shack: Where Tragedy Confronts Eternity*

Questions

- When do you find it difficult to "submit"?
- In what areas of your life do you think it is important to "submit"?

© 2015 National Association of Christian Women Entrepreneurs * All Rights Reserved * www.nacwe.org

NACWE Word of the Week: Study and Discussion
January 19. 2015

The Word of the Week is: Transformation

Definition- Transformation
‚tran(t)sfərˈmāSH(ə)n/
noun
- a thorough or dramatic change in form or appearance.

synonyms: change, alteration, mutation, conversion, metamorphosis, transfiguration, transmutation,

Scripture

Romans 12:2 Do not be conformed to this world, but be transformed by the renewal of your mind, that by testing you may discern what is the will of God, what is good and acceptable and perfect.

2 Corinthians 3:18 And we all, with unveiled face, beholding the glory of the Lord, are being transformed into the same image from one degree of glory to another. For this comes from the Lord who is the Spirit.

Quotation

"Transformation is a process, and as life happens there are tons of ups and downs. It's a journey of discovery - there are moments on mountaintops and moments in deep valleys of despair." Rick Warren

Questions

- In the last year, where have you seen areas of transformation in your life? Tell us about them.
- How does God want you be transformed this year? Spiritually, Relationally, Financially, Physically, Vocationally, Mentally?

© 2015 National Association of Christian Women Entrepreneurs * All Rights Reserved * www.nacwe.org

NACWE Word of the Week: Study and Discussion

January 26. 2015

The Word of the Week is: Healthy

Definition- Healthy
/ˈhelTHē/
adjective
- in good health.

synonyms: Well, in good health, fine, fit, in good trim, in good shape, in fine fettle, in tip-top shape, Blooming, thriving, hardy, robust, strong, vigorous

Scripture

Proverbs 3:8 This will bring health to your body and nourishment to your bones.

Psalm 26:2 Test me Lord, and try me, examine my heart and my mind.

1 Chronicles 6:19 Don't you realize that your body is the temple of the Holy Spirit, who lives in you and was given to you by God? You do not belong to yourself,

Quotation

"There's a difference between interest and commitment. When you're interested in doing something, you only do it when it is convenient. When you are committed to something, you accept no excuses; only results." ~Kenneth Blanchard

Questions

- What areas in your life do you need to improve the health on: mindset, body, spiritual, business?
- Over the years what area has been the toughest to improve the health of? Why was it so hard, was there something you were holding tight to that needed to be released? Or perhaps something you were/are avoiding to change because it was to hard?

© 2015 National Association of Christian Women Entrepreneurs * All Rights Reserved * www.nacwe.org

NACWE Word of the Week: Study and Discussion
February 2, 2015

The Word of the Week is: Renew(al)

Definition- Renew
rəˈn(y)o͞o/
verb
- resume (an activity) after an interruption.

    synonyms: resume, return to, take up again, come back to, begin again, start again, restart, recommence;
- re-establish (a relationship).

Scripture
Psalms 51:10-12
Create in me a clean heart, O God, And renew a steadfast spirit within me. Do not cast me away from Your presence And do not take Your Holy Spirit from me. Restore to me the joy of Your salvation And sustain me with a willing spirit.

Romans 12:2
And do not be conformed to this world, but be transformed by the renewing of your mind, so that you may prove what the will of God is, that which is good and acceptable and perfect.

Ephesians 4:22-24
You were taught, with regard to your former way of life, to put off your old self, which is being corrupted by its deceitful desires; to be made new in the attitude of your minds; and to put on the new self, created to be like God in true righteousness and holiness.

Quotation
"Renewal requires opening yourself up to new ways of thinking and feeling"
― Deborah Day, BE HAPPY NOW!

Questions
- Where do you see renewal happening in your life? Where does it need to happen?
- What bible verses mean the most to you about the word renew or renewal?

© 2015 National Association of Christian Women Entrepreneurs * All Rights Reserved * www.nacwe.org

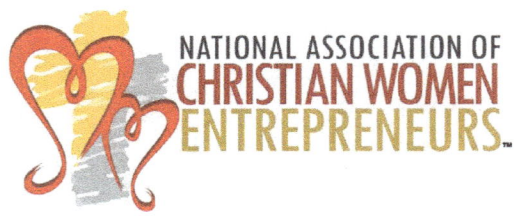

NACWE Word of the Week: Study and Discussion
February 9, 2015

The Word of the Week is: Bold

Definition
Bold
adjective
1. (of a person, action, or idea) showing an ability to take risks; confident and courageous.

synonyms: daring, intrepid, brave, courageous, valiant, valorous, fearless, dauntless, audacious, daredevil;

2. (of a color or design) having a strong or vivid appearance.

synonyms: striking, vivid, bright, strong, eye-catching, prominent, impactful; More

Scripture

Psalms 138:3
On the day I called, You answered me; You made me bold with strength in my soul.

2 Corinthians 3:12
Therefore having such a hope, we use great boldness in our speech,

Exodus 14:8
The LORD hardened the heart of Pharaoh, king of Egypt, and he chased after the sons of Israel as the sons of Israel were going out boldly.

Quotation
"Past boldness is no assurance of future boldness. Boldness demands continual reliance on God's spirit." — Andy Stanley

Questions

- Where do you need to be bold or bolder in your life?
- What tools do you use to help you learn to be bold?
- Find a quote or a bible verse that speaks to you about being bold.

May God bless your week!!

© 2015 National Association of Christian Women Entrepreneurs * All Rights Reserved * www.nacwe.org

NACWE Word of the Week: Study and Discussion
January 26. 2015

The Word of the Week is: CONNECT

Definition- CONNECT

con·nect
kəˈnekt/
verb
verb: **connect**; 3rd person present: **connects**; past tense: **connected**; past participle: **connected**; gerund or present participle: **connecting**

1. bring together or into contact so that a real or notional link is established.

   "the electrodes were **connected to** a recording device"

   synonyms: attach, join, fasten, fix, affix, couple, link, secure, hitch; More stick, adhere, fuse, pin, screw, bolt, clamp, clip, hook (up); add, append
   "electrodes were connected to the device"

   o join together so as to provide access and communication.

      "all the buildings are connected by underground passages"

   o link to a power or water supply.

      "your house is **connected to** the main cable TV network"

Scripture

The Bible says that that being spiritually connected means:

- Ephesians 2:22 ... **We're built like a building.** "In Him you also are being built together into a dwelling place for God by the Spirit."
- Romans 12:4-5 ... **We're joined in a body.** "⁴ For as in one body we have many members,[e] and the members do not all have the same function, ⁵ so we, though many, are one body in Christ, and individually members one of another."

© 2015 National Association of Christian Women Entrepreneurs * All Rights Reserved * www.nacwe.org

NACWE Word of the Week: Study and Discussion
February 23, 2015

The Word of the Week is: JOY

Definition of Joy

Noun
a feeling of great pleasure and happiness.
synonyms: delight, great
pleasure, joyfulness, jubilation, triumph, exultation, rejoicing, happiness, gladness, glee, exhilaration, exuberance, elation, euphoria, bliss, ecstasy, rapture

Scripture

Galatians 5:22 But the fruit of the Spirit is love, **joy**, peace, forbearance, kindness, goodness, faithfulness

Nehemiah 8:10 …the **joy** of the LORD is your strength.

James 1:2-3 Consider it pure **joy**, my brothers and sisters, whenever you face trials of many kinds, because you know that the testing of your faith produces perseverance.

Quotation

"Joy is the settled assurance that God is in control of all the details of my life, the quiet confidence that ultimately everything is going to be all right, and the determined choice to praise God in all things." **Kay Warren**

Questions

- Do you think the feeling of joy is a choice?
- Is happiness the same thing as joy?
- What can you do to have more joy in your life?

May God bless your week!!

© 2015 National Association of Christian Women Entrepreneurs * All Rights Reserved * www.nacwe.org

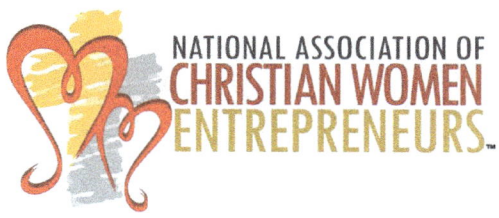

NACWE Word of the Week: Study and Discussion
March 2, 2015

The Word of the Week is: Shine

Definition- Shine

1. brightness caused by the emission of light
2. brightness caused by the reflection of light :
3. brilliance, splendor

Synonyms- burnish, gloss, luminance, luster (or lustre), polish, sheen

Scripture

Matthew 5:16 "In the same way, let your light **shine** before others, that they may see your good deeds and glorify your Father in heaven."

Isaiah 60:1 "Arise, **shine**, for your light has come, and the glory of the LORD rises upon you."

Daniel 12:3 "Those who are wise will **shine** like the brightness of the heavens, and those who lead many to righteousness, like the stars for ever and ever."

Quotation

"We are told to let our light shine, and if it does, we won't need to tell anybody it does. Lighthouses don't fire cannons to call attention to their shining- they just shine."
Dwight L. Moody

"Never dull your shine for somebody else." — Tyra Banks

Questions

- How do you see the word "shine" as significant in your life?
- Is it hard for you to "shine"? Why or why not?

© 2015 National Association of Christian Women Entrepreneurs * All Rights Reserved * www.nacwe.org

NACWE Word of the Week: Study and Discussion

March 9, 2015

The Word of the Week is: LOVE

Definition-Love
noun
1. an intense feeling of deep affection.

synonyms: deep affection, fondness, tenderness, warmth, intimacy, attachment, endearment

2. a person or thing that one loves.

synonyms: beloved, loved one, love of one's life, dear, dearest, dear one, darling, sweetheart, sweet, angel, honey

Scripture

John 3:16 For God so loved the world that he gave his one and only Son, that whoever believes in him shall not perish but have eternal life.

Matthew 22:37-39 Jesus replied: "'Love the Lord your God with all your heart and with all your soul and with all your mind. This is the first and greatest commandment. And the second is like it: 'Love your neighbor as yourself'.

1 Corinthian 13:13 And now these three remain: faith, hope and love. But the greatest of these is love.

Quotation
"Love all, trust a few, do wrong to none."   William Shakespeare, *All's Well That Ends Well*

Questions
- Are there people you have trouble showing love?   What do you do?
- How do you follow God's greatest commandment?
- Will you try to show love to one person this week that you have struggled to show love to in the past?

May God bless your week!!

© 2015 National Association of Christian Women Entrepreneurs * All Rights Reserved * www.nacwe.org

NACWE Word of the Week: Study and Discussion
March 16, 2015

The Word of the Week is: TRUST

Definition-Trust
noun
firm belief in the reliability, truth, ability, or strength of someone or something.
synonyms: confidence, belief, faith, certainty, assurance, conviction, credence, reliance

verb
believe in the reliability, truth, ability, or strength of.
synonyms: rely on, depend on, bank on, count on, be sure of

Scripture
Proverbs 3:5-6 Trust in the LORD with all your heart and lean not on your own understanding; in all your ways acknowledge him, and he will make your paths straight.

John 14:1 "Do not let your hearts be troubled. Trust in God; trust also in me.

Quotation
"Whoever is careless with the truth in small matters cannot be trusted with important matters." --*Albert Einstein*

Questions
- Is it hard for you to trust people?
- Is it hard for you to trust God?
- How does a person learn to trust God?
- Do you agree with this statement? "Trust is a valued character trait often lacking in today's world. We have to learn to trust God in every circumstance and in every area of our lives."

May God bless your week!!

© 2015 National Association of Christian Women Entrepreneurs * All Rights Reserved * www.nacwe.org

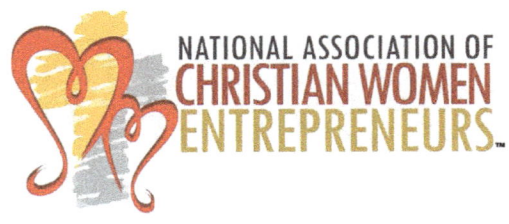

NACWE Word of the Week: Study and Discussion

March 23, 2015

The Word of the Week is: Humility

Definition-Humility
noun
1. the quality or condition of being humble; modest opinion or estimate of one's own importance, rank, etc.

Synonyms: lowliness, meekness, submissiveness.
Antonyms: pride

Scripture
Proverbs 11:2 When pride comes, then comes disgrace, but with humility comes wisdom.
Ephesians 4:2 Be completely humble and gentle; be patient, bearing with one another in love.
James 3:13 Who is wise and understanding among you? Let them show it by their good life, by deeds done in the humility that comes from wisdom.

Quotation
"Humility is the mother of all virtues; purity, charity and obedience. It is in being humble that our love becomes real, devoted and ardent. If you are humble nothing will touch you, neither praise nor disgrace, because you know what you are. If you are blamed you will not be discouraged. If they call you a saint you will not put yourself on a pedestal."
Mother Teresa

Questions
- How hard is it for you to practice humility?
- Have you read proverbs? Glance through Proverbs and see how many verses talk about humility.

May God bless your week!!

© 2015 National Association of Christian Women Entrepreneurs * All Rights Reserved * www.nacwe.org

NACWE Word of the Week: Study and Discussion
March 30, 2015

The Word of the Week is: Sacrifice

Definition- **Sacrifice**

1. the act of giving up something that you want to keep especially in order to get or do something else or to help someone
2. an act of killing a person or animal in a religious ceremony as an offering to please a god
3. a person or animal that is killed in a sacrifice

Scripture

Proverbs 21:3 To do what is right and just is more acceptable to the Lord than sacrifice.
Ephesians 5:2 ...and walk in the way of love, just as Christ loved us and gave himself up for us as a fragrant offering and sacrifice to God.
Hebrews 9:28 So Christ was sacrificed once to take away the sins of many; and he will appear a second time, not to bear sin, but to bring salvation to those who are waiting for him.

Quotation

"Great achievement is usually born of great sacrifice, and is never the result of selfishness." *Napoleon Hill*

"There's only one effectively redemptive sacrifice, the sacrifice of self-will to make room for the knowledge of God." *Aldous Huxley*

Questions

John 3:16 For God so loved the world that he gave [sacrificed] his one and only Son, that whoever believes in him shall not perish but have eternal life. What does this mean for you?
Please meditate on this scripture this week during Holy Week.

Have a blessed week!

© 2015 National Association of Christian Women Entrepreneurs * All Rights Reserved * www.nacwe.org

NACWE Word of the Week: Study and Discussion
April 6, 2015

The Word of the Week is: Redeemed

Definition-Redeemed
verb
past tense: **redeemed**; past participle: **redeemed**
1. compensate for the faults or bad aspects of (something).
synonyms: save, compensate for the defects of, vindicate
2. gain or regain possession of (something) in exchange for payment.
synonyms: retrieve, regain, recover, get back, reclaim, repossess;
    buy back

Scripture
Colossians 1:13-14 "He delivered us from the power of darkness and transferred us to the kingdom of His beloved Son, in whom we have redemption, the forgiveness of sins."

Ephesians 1:7-10 "In Him we have redemption by His blood, the forgiveness of transgressions, in accord with the riches of His grace that He lavished upon us. In all wisdom and insight, He has made known to us the mystery of His will in accord with His favor that He set forth in Him as a plan for the fullness of times, to sum up all things in Christ, in heaven and on earth."

Quotation
"Redemption is not perfection. The redeemed must realize their imperfections."
John Piper

Questions
- What does being redeemed mean to you?
- Are you redeemed?
- Is anyone else redeemed because of you?

May God bless your week and Happy Easter!

© 2015 National Association of Christian Women Entrepreneurs * All Rights Reserved * www.nacwe.org

NACWE Word of the Week: Study and Discussion
April 13, 2015

The Word of the Week is: Persistence

Definition-Persistence
Noun
1. the quality that allows someone to continue doing something or trying to do something even though it is difficult or opposed by other people
2. the state of occurring or existing beyond the usual, expected, or normal time

Synonyms
abidance, ceaselessness, continuance, continuity, continuousness, durability, duration, endurance, continuation, subsistence, perseverance

Scripture

[Galatians 6:9](#) And let us not grow weary of doing good, for in due season we will reap, if we do not give up.

[1 Thessalonians 5:17](#) Pray without ceasing,

[1 Corinthians 15:58](#) Therefore, my beloved brothers, be steadfast, immovable, always abounding in the work of the Lord, knowing that in the Lord your labor is not in vain.

Quotation
"It's not that I'm so smart, it's just that I stay with problems longer." *Albert Einstein*

Questions
- Are you persistent?
- What helps you persist in your endeavors?
- What keeps you from being persistent?

May God bless your week!

© 2015 National Association of Christian Women Entrepreneurs * All Rights Reserved * www.nacwe.org

NACWE Word of the Week: Study and Discussion

April 21, 2015

The Word of the Week is: Compassion

Definition- **Compassion**

Noun
Sympathetic pity and concern for the sufferings or misfortunes of others.

synonyms: pity, sympathy, empathy, fellow feeling, care, concern, solicitude, sensitivity, warmth, love, tenderness, mercy, leniency, tolerance, kindness, humanity, charity

Scripture

2 Corinthians 1:3-4 Blessed be the God and Father of our Lord Jesus Christ, the Father of mercies and God of all comfort, who comforts us in all our affliction, so that we may be able to comfort those who are in any affliction, with the comfort with which we ourselves are comforted by God.

Matthew 9:36 When he saw the crowds, he had compassion for them, because they were harassed and helpless, like sheep without a shepherd.

Quotation

"All major religious traditions carry basically the same message, that is love, compassion and forgiveness the important thing is they should be part of our daily lives." *Dalai Lama*

Questions

- Do you have compassion for others?
- What could you do to feel and/or show more compassion for people and situations?

Have a blessed week!

© 2015 National Association of Christian Women Entrepreneurs * All Rights Reserved * www.nacwe.org

NACWE Word of the Week: Study and Discussion
April 27, 2015

The Word of the Week is Action

Definition- **Action**

noun
1. the fact or process of doing something, typically to achieve an aim.
synonyms: measures, steps, activity, movement, work, operation
   "the need for local community action"

2. a thing done; an act.
synonyms: deed, act, move, undertaking, exploit, maneuver, endeavor, effort, exertion

Scripture

<u>Colossians 3:23-24</u> Whatever you do, work heartily, as for the Lord and not for men, knowing that from the Lord you will receive the inheritance as your reward. You are serving the Lord Jesus Christ.

<u>Luke 11:9</u> And I tell you, ask, and it will be given to you; seek, and you will find; knock, and it will be opened to you.

<u>1 Peter 1:13</u> Therefore, preparing your minds for action, and being sober-minded, set your hope fully on the grace that will be brought to you at the revelation of Jesus Christ.

Quotation

"Take action. Try new things. Be willing to be very uncomfortable and rather frightened on a regular basis. This is how you will build a business, but more importantly build a magnificent, brave, authentic life." *Diane Cunningham*

Questions
- Do you take action?
- What drives you?
- What impedes your action taking?

Have a blessed week!

© 2015 National Association of Christian Women Entrepreneurs * All Rights Reserved * www.nacwe.org

NACWE Word of the Week: Study and Discussion
May 4. 2015

The Word of the Week is: Encourage

Definition- Encourage
inˈkərij/ *verb*

To give support, confidence, or hope to (someone).

synonyms: hearten, cheer, buoy up, uplift, inspire, motivate, spur on, stir, stir up, fire up, stimulate, invigorate, vitalize, revitalize, embolden, fortify, rally, pep up, promising, hopeful, auspicious, propitious, favorable, bright, rosy; heartening, reassuring, cheering, comforting, welcome, pleasing, understanding, helpful; positive, responsive, enthusiastic, boosterish

Scripture

Proverbs 10:21 The words of the godly encourage, many, but fools are destroyed by their lack of common sense..

Romans 1:12 When we get together, I want to encourage you in your faith, but I also want to be encouraged by yours.

Romans 14:19 So then, let us aim for harmony in the church and try to build each other up

1 Corinthians 14:12 Even so you, since you are zealous for spiritual gifts, let it be for the edification of the church that you seek to excel.

Quotation

"You don't have to knock anyone off their game to win yours. It doesn't build you up to tear others down." ~Mandy Hale

Questions

- Do you build others up on a regular basis?
- What stops you from encouraging and edifying other women?
- How can you encourage someone today?
- How have you felt when someone encouraged or edified you?
- What ways can you edify/encourage other women in the Lord?

© 2015 National Association of Christian Women Entrepreneurs * All Rights Reserved * www.nacwe.org

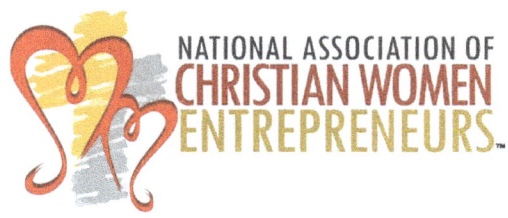

NACWE Word of the Week: Study and Discussion

May 11, 2015

The Word of the Week is Diligence

Definition- **Diligence**

noun
careful and persistent work or effort.
synonyms: conscientiousness, assiduousness, assiduity, hard work, application, concentration, effort, care, industriousness, rigor, meticulousness, thoroughness, perseverance, persistence, tenacity, dedication, commitment, tirelessness, indefatigability, doggedness

Scripture

Proverbs 21:5 The plans of the diligent lead surely to advantage, But everyone who is hasty comes surely to poverty.

1 Corinthians 15:58 Therefore, my beloved brethren, be steadfast, immovable, always abounding in the work of the Lord, knowing that your toil is not in vain in the Lord.

Galatians 6:9 Let us not lose heart in doing good, for in due time we will reap if we do not grow weary.

Quotation

"The expectations of life depend upon diligence; the mechanic that would perfect his work must first sharpen his tools." *Confucius*

Questions
- Are you diligent in your work?
- Are you diligent in pursuing a relationship with God?
- What could you do to be more diligent in both of these areas?

Have a blessed week!

© 2015 National Association of Christian Women Entrepreneurs * All Rights Reserved * www.nacwe.org

NACWE Word of the Week: Study and Discussion

May 18, 2015

The Word of the Week is Desire

Definition- **Desire**

noun
1. a strong feeling of wanting to have something or wishing for something to happen.
synonyms: wish, want, aspiration, fancy, inclination, impulse

verb
2. strongly wish for or want (something).
synonyms: want, wish for, long for, yearn for, crave, hanker after, be desperate for, be bent on, covet, aspire to; fancy

Scripture

Psalm 37:4 Take delight in the LORD, and he will give you the desires of your heart. NIV

1 John 2:17 The world and its desires pass away, but whoever does the will of God lives forever. NIV

Proverbs 13:2 Hope deferred makes the heart sick, but a longing fulfilled is a tree of life. NIV

Quotation

"Desire is the starting point of all achievement, not a hope, not a wish, but a keen pulsating desire which transcends everything." *Napoleon Hill*

Questions

- What are your heart's desires?
- Are you pursuing your heart's desires?
- What is helping or holding you back?

Have a blessed week!

© 2015 National Association of Christian Women Entrepreneurs * All Rights Reserved * www.nacwe.org

NACWE Word of the Week: Study and Discussion
May 25. 2015

The Word of the Week is: Grace

Definition- Grace
/grās/ noun

(in Christian belief) the free and unmerited favor of God, as manifested in the salvation of sinners and the bestowal of blessings.

synonyms: dignify, distinguish, honor, favor; enhance, ennoble, glorify, elevate,

Scripture

Psalm 84:11 For the LORD God is our sun and our shield. He gives us **grace** and glory. The LORD will withhold no good thing from those who do what is right.

Acts 15:11 We believe that we are all saved the same way, by the undeserved **grace** of the Lord Jesus."

Romans 6:14 Sin is no longer your master, for you no longer live under the requirements of the law. Instead, you live under the freedom of God's **grace**.

Hebrews 4:16 So let us come boldly to the throne of our gracious God. There we will receive his mercy, and we will find grace to help us when we need it most.

Quotation
What gives me the most hope every day is God's grace; knowing that his grace is going to give me the strength for whatever I face, knowing that nothing is a surprise to God.
~Rick Warren

Questions
- How do you define grace today?
- Have you shown grace to someone that did not deserve it?
- Have you been shown grace by someone?

© 2015 National Association of Christian Women Entrepreneurs * All Rights Reserved * www.nacwe.org

NACWE Word of the Week: Study and Discussion

June 1, 2015

The Word of the Week is: Passion

Definition- Passion
pas·sion

ˈpaSHən/noun

An intense desire or enthusiasm for something, a thing arousing enthusiasm. (Also mentions Passion of the Christ movie)

synonyms:
fervor, ardor, enthusiasm, eagerness, zeal, zealousness, vigor, fire, fieriness, energy, fervency, animation, spirit, spiritedness,

Scripture

Galatians 4:18 But it is good to be **zealous** in a good thing always, and not only when I am present with you.

1 Corinthians 14:12 Even so you, since you are **zealous** for spiritual gifts, let it be for the edification of the church that you seek to excel.

Romans 12:11 Never be lacking in **zeal**, but keep your spiritual **fervor**, serving the Lord.

Colossians 1:29 To this end I strenuously contend with all the **energy** Christ so powerfully works in me.

Quotation

A great leader's courage to fulfill his vision comes from passion, not position.   ~John C. Maxwell

Questions

- What are you passionate about?
- What drives your passion?
- How can you fan the fire of your passion?

© 2015 National Association of Christian Women Entrepreneurs * All Rights Reserved * www.nacwe.org

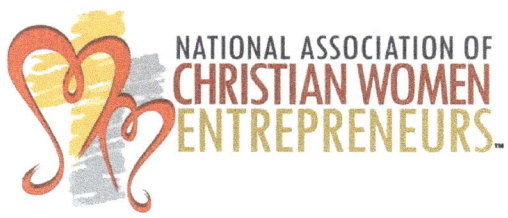

NACWE Word of the Week: Study and Discussion

June 8, 2015

The Word of the Week is Prayer

Definition- **Prayer**

noun
a solemn request for help or expression of thanks addressed to God or an object of worship.

Scripture

Ephesians 6:18 *praying at all times in the Spirit, with all prayer and supplication. To that end keep alert with all perseverance, making supplication for all the saints,*

Mark 11:24 *Therefore I tell you, whatever you ask in prayer, believe that you have received it, and it will be yours.*

Philippians 4:6-7 *do not be anxious about anything, but in everything by prayer and supplication with thanksgiving let your requests be made known to God. And the peace of God, which surpasses all understanding, will guard your hearts and your minds in Christ Jesus.*

Quotation

Don't pray when you feel like it. Have an appointment with the Lord and keep it. A man is powerful on his knees. ~ *Corrie Ten Boom*

Questions

- Do you pray about everything?
- Think about the times God has answered your prayers, and thank Him for His answer.

Have a blessed week!

© 2015 National Association of Christian Women Entrepreneurs * All Rights Reserved * www.nacwe.org

NACWE Word of the Week: Study and Discussion

June 15, 2015

The Word of the Week is Fear

Definition- **Fear**

noun
1. an unpleasant emotion caused by the belief that someone or something is dangerous, likely to cause pain, or a threat.

synonyms: terror, fright, fearfulness, horror, alarm, panic, agitation, trepidation, dread, consternation, dismay, distress

verb
2. be afraid of (someone or something) as likely to be dangerous, painful, or threatening.

Scripture

Isaiah 41:10 So do not fear, for I am with you; do not be dismayed, for I am your God. I will strengthen you and help you; I will uphold you with my righteous right hand. **NIV**

1 John 4:18 There is no fear in love. But perfect love drives out fear, because fear has to do with punishment. The one who fears is not made perfect in love. **NIV**

Psalm 23:4 Even though I walk through the darkest valley, I will fear no evil, for you are with me; your rod and your staff, they comfort me. **NIV**

Quotation

"**FEAR**, **F**alse **E**vidence **A**ppearing **R**eal"...Unknown

Questions

- What is your greatest fear?
- What do you do when fear threatens you?
- Do you know how many verses in the bible are about fear???

Have a blessed week!

© 2015 National Association of Christian Women Entrepreneurs * All Rights Reserved * www.nacwe.org

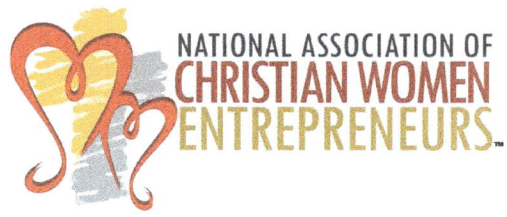

NACWE Word of the Week: Study and Discussion
June 22, 2015

The Word of the Week is Imagination

Definition- **Imagination**

noun
- the faculty or action of forming new ideas, or images or concepts of external objects not present to the senses.
  synonyms: creative power, fancy, vision
- the ability of the mind to be creative or resourceful
  synonyms: creativity, imaginativeness, creativeness
- the part of the mind that imagines things.

Scripture

Ephesians 1:17-18 ESV That the God of our Lord Jesus Christ, the Father of glory, may give you a spirit of wisdom and of revelation in the knowledge of him, having the eyes of your hearts enlightened, that you may know what is the hope to which he has called you, what are the riches of his glorious inheritance in the saints...

2 Corinthians 10:5 KJV Casting down imaginations, and every high thing that exalteth itself against the knowledge of God, and bringing into captivity every thought to the obedience of Christ;

1 Corinthians 2:9 NIV However, as it is written: "What no eye has seen, what no ear has heard, and what no human mind has conceived"— the things God has prepared for those who love him—

Quotation

" Imagination is more important than knowledge. Knowledge is limited. Imagination encircles the world." *Albert Einstein*

Questions

- Do you have an imagination? How has it helped you in life and/or in your business?
- In what areas would you like to have a more active imagination?
- Do you imagine what heaven will be like?

© 2015 National Association of Christian Women Entrepreneurs * All Rights Reserved * www.nacwe.org

NACWE Word of the Week: Study and Discussion
June 29, 2015

The Word of the Week is VICTORY

Definition- **VICTORY**

Noun
- an act of defeating an enemy or opponent in a battle, game, or other competition.

synonyms: success, triumph, conquest, win, favorable result; landslide, coup; mastery, superiority, supremacy

Scripture

Deuteronomy 20:4 NIV For the LORD your God is the one who goes with you to fight for you against your enemies to give you victory.

Proverbs 21:31 NIV The horse is made ready for the day of battle, but victory rests with the LORD.

1 Corinthian 15:37 NIV But thanks be to God! He gives us the victory through our Lord Jesus Christ.

Quotation

"Great victory requires great risk.-Hera" — Rick Riordan, *The Lost Hero*

Questions

- Do you feel victorious? Why or why not?
- What can you do to live a life of victory?

God Bless Your Week!

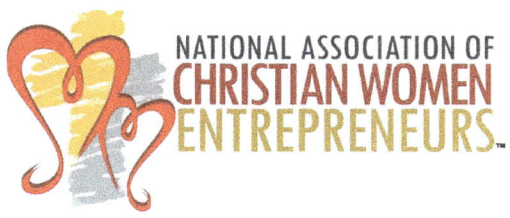

NACWE Word of the Week: Study and Discussion
July 6, 2015

The Word of the Week is SHARPEN

Definition- **SHARPEN**

verb
 1. make or become sharp.
synonyms: hone, whet, strop, grind, file

 2. improve or cause to improve.
synonyms: improve, brush up, polish up, better, enhance;
    hone, fine-tune, perfect

Scripture

Proverbs 27:17 NIV As iron sharpens iron, so one person sharpens another.

Ecclesiastes 10:10 NASB If the axe is dull and he does not sharpen its edge, then he must exert more strength. Wisdom has the advantage of giving success.

Psalms 64:3 NASB Who have sharpened their tongue like a sword They aimed bitter speech as their arrow,

Quotation

"The expectations of life depend upon diligence; the mechanic that would perfect his work must first sharpen his tools." *Confucius*

Questions

- How much time to you spend sharpening your "tools"…in your life and in your business?
- What methods do you use to sharpen yourself?

God Bless Your Week!

© 2015 National Association of Christian Women Entrepreneurs * All Rights Reserved * www.nacwe.org

NACWE Word of the Week: Study and Discussion
July 13, 2015

The Word of the Week is ABIDE

Definition- **ABIDE**

Verb

accept or act in accordance with (a rule, decision, or recommendation).
synonyms: comply with, obey, observe, follow, keep to, hold to, conform to, adhere to, stick to, stand by, act in accordance with, uphold, heed, accept, go along with, acknowledge, respect, defer to

Scripture

John 15:4-9 NASB Abide in Me, and I in you. As the branch cannot bear fruit of itself unless it abides in the vine, so neither can you unless you abide in Me. "I am the vine, you are the branches; he who abides in Me and I in him, he bears much fruit, for apart from Me you can do nothing. "If anyone does not abide in Me, he is thrown away as a branch and dries up; and they gather them, and cast them into the fire and they are burned. If you abide in Me, and My words abide in you, ask whatever you wish, and it will be done for you. "My Father is glorified by this, that you bear much fruit, and so prove to be My disciples. "Just as the Father has loved Me, I have also loved you; abide in My love.

Quotation

"We cannot abide in the Word of God and not be moved to action. We cannot sit on the sidelines. Like David, who ran to the front lines, we'll be looking for giants to conquer."
Mark Batterson, Draw the Circle, Day 30

Questions

- How do you "abide" in Jesus?
- What does 'abiding in Jesus" mean to you?
- How has abiding in Jesus moved you to action?

God Bless Your Week!

© 2015 National Association of Christian Women Entrepreneurs * All Rights Reserved * www.nacwe.org

NACWE Word of the Week: Study and Discussion
July 20, 2015

The Word of the Week is COMPASSION

Definition- **COMPASSION**

noun
- sympathetic pity and concern for the sufferings or misfortunes of others.

synonyms: pity, sympathy, empathy, fellow feeling, care, concern, solicitude, sensitivity, warmth, love, tenderness, mercy, leniency, tolerance, kindness, humanity, charity
- deep awareness of the suffering of another accompanied by the wish to relieve it

Scripture

Matthew 14:14 When he went ashore he saw a great crowd, and he had compassion on them and healed their sick.

Colossians 3:12-13 Put on then, as God's chosen ones, holy and beloved, compassionate hearts, kindness, humility, meekness, and patience, bearing with one another and, if one has a complaint against another, forgiving each other; as the Lord has forgiven you, so you also must forgive.

1 Peter 3:8 Finally, all of you, have unity of mind, sympathy, brotherly love, a tender heart, and a humble mind.

Quotation

"Until he extends the circle of his compassion to all living things, man will not himself find peace." *Albert Schweitzer*

Questions

- Do you have compassion?
- Do you have to work at having compassion?
- What is the most important thing to you in regard to having compassion?

May God Bless Your Week!!

© 2015 National Association of Christian Women Entrepreneurs * All Rights Reserved * www.nacwe.org

NACWE Word of the Week: Study and Discussion
July 27, 2015

The Word of the Week is PRIDE

Definition- **PRIDE**

noun
1. a feeling or deep pleasure or satisfaction derived from one's own achievements, the achievements of those with whom one is closely associated, or from qualities or possessions that are widely admired.

synonyms: pleasure, joy, delight, gratification, fulfillment, satisfaction, a sense of achievement

verb
1. be especially proud of a particular quality or skill.

Scripture

Galatians 6:4 NIV Each one should test his own actions. Then he can take pride in himself, without comparing himself to somebody else, for each one should carry his own load.
Proverbs 13:10 NIV Pride only breeds quarrels, but wisdom is found in those who take advice.
Ecclesiastes 7:8 NIV The end of a matter is better than its beginning, and patience is better than pride.

Quotation

"It is better to lose your pride with someone you love rather than to lose that someone you love with your useless pride." *John Ruskin*

Questions

- Do you struggle with pride?
- What do you do to combat feelings of pride in your life?

May God Bless Your Week!!

© 2015 National Association of Christian Women Entrepreneurs * All Rights Reserved * www.nacwe.org

NACWE Word of the Week: Study and Discussion
August 3, 2015

The Word of the Week is HOPE

Definition- **HOPE**

noun
1. a feeling of expectation and desire for a certain thing to happen.

synonyms: aspiration, desire, wish, expectation, ambition, aim, goal, plan, design; dream, daydream, pipe dream

verb
1. want something to happen or be the case.

synonyms: expect, anticipate, look for, be hopeful of, pin one's hopes on, want; wish for, long for, dream of

Scripture

Jeremiah 29:11 For I know the thoughts that I think toward you, says the LORD, thoughts of peace and not of evil, to give you a future and a hope.

Isaiah 9:7 This life can beat us down with trials, sorrows and debilitating worries. When it seems hopeless, God's messages about our future hope can deeply encourage us.

Titus 3:7 So that being justified by his grace we might become heirs according to the hope of eternal life.

Quotation

"The very least you can do in your life is to figure out what you hope for. And the most you can do is live inside that hope. Not admire it from a distance but live right in it, under its roof." *Barbara Kingsolver*

Questions

- What is your greatest hope?
- How do you keep hope alive on bad days?

May God bless each of you!

© 2015 National Association of Christian Women Entrepreneurs * All Rights Reserved * www.nacwe.org

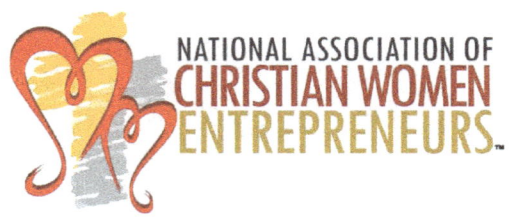

NACWE Word of the Week: Study and Discussion
August 10, 2015

The Word of the Week is MERCY

Definition- **MERCY**

noun
1. compassion or forgiveness shown toward someone whom it is within one's power to punish or harm.

synonyms: leniency, clemency, compassion, grace, pity, charity, forgiveness, forbearance, quarter, humanity

exclamation
archaic
1. used in expressions of surprise or fear.

Scripture

Psalms 86:5 For you, Lord, are good, and ready to forgive; and plenteous in mercy to all them that call on you.

Ephesians 2:4 But God, who is rich in mercy, for his great love with which he loved us,

Hebrews 4:16 Let us therefore come boldly to the throne of grace, that we may obtain mercy, and find grace to help in time of need.

Quotation

"God's mercy is fresh and new every morning." *Joyce Meyer*

Questions

- How has God shown mercy to you?
- Do you have difficulty showing mercy to others? Do you know why?

May God Bless Your Week!!

© 2015 National Association of Christian Women Entrepreneurs * All Rights Reserved * www.nacwe.org

NACWE Word of the Week: Study and Discussion
August 17, 2015

The Word of the Week is EMPOWER

Definition- **EMPOWER**

verb
1. give (someone) the authority or power to do something.

synonyms: authorize, entitle, permit, allow, license, sanction, warrant, commission, delegate, qualify, enable, equip

2. make (someone) stronger and more confident, especially in controlling their life and claiming their rights.

synonyms: emancipate, unshackle, set free, liberate

Scripture

Deuteronomy 31:6 ESV Be strong and courageous. Do not fear or be in dread of them, for it is the Lord your God who goes with you. He will not leave you or forsake you.

2 Corinthians 12:9 ESV But he said to me, "My grace is sufficient for you, for my power is made perfect in weakness." Therefore I will boast all the more gladly of my weaknesses, so that the power of Christ may rest upon me.

Matthew 28:18-20 ESV And Jesus came and said to them, "All authority in heaven and on earth has been given to me. Go therefore and make disciples of all nations, baptizing them in the name of the Father and of the Son and of the Holy Spirit, teaching them to observe all that I have commanded you. And behold, I am with you always, to the end of the age."

Quotation

"Leaders become great, not because of their power, but because of their ability to empower others." *John Maxwell*

Questions

- What helps you to feel empowered?
- How do you help others to feel empowered?

© 2015 National Association of Christian Women Entrepreneurs * All Rights Reserved * www.nacwe.org

NACWE Word of the Week: Study and Discussion
August 24, 2015

The Word of the Week is COVENANT

Definition- **COVENANT**

noun
1. an agreement.

synonyms: contract, agreement, undertaking, commitment, guarantee, warrant, pledge, promise, bond, indenture; pact, deal, settlement, arrangement, understanding

verb
1. agree, especially by lease, deed, or other legal contract.

synonyms: undertake, contract, guarantee, pledge, promise, agree, engage, warrant, commit oneself, bind oneself

Scripture

Ephesians 2:12-13 "...at that time [before the cross] you were without Christ, being aliens from the commonwealth of Israel and strangers from the covenants of promise, having no hope and without God in the world. But now in Christ Jesus you who once were far off have been brought near by the blood of Christ."

Hebrews 13:20-21 "Now may the God of peace who brought up our Lord Jesus from the dead, that great Shepherd of the sheep, through the blood of the everlasting covenant, make you complete in every good work to do His will, working in you what is well pleasing in His sight, through Jesus Christ, to whom be glory forever and ever. Amen."

Quotation

"God doesn't want us to have rigid rituals with Him. In the new covenant, He is more interested in having a relationship with us." *Joseph Prince*

Questions

- What does God's covenant mean to you?
- How has God's covenant through Christ changed or impacted your life?

May God Bless Your Week!!

© 2015 National Association of Christian Women Entrepreneurs * All Rights Reserved * www.nacwe.org

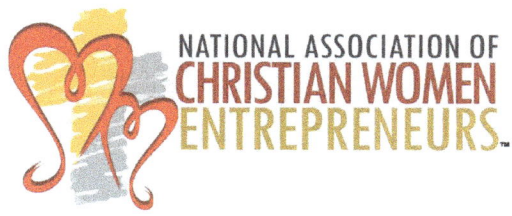

NACWE Word of the Week: Study and Discussion
August 31, 2015

The Word of the Week is FORGIVENESS

Definition- **FORGIVENESS**

noun
1. the action or process of forgiving or being forgiven.

synonyms: pardon, absolution, exoneration, remission, dispensation, indulgence, clemency, mercy, reprieve, amnesty

Scripture

Psalm 86:4-5 Gladden the soul of your servant, for to you, O Lord, do I lift up my soul. For you, O Lord, are good and forgiving, abounding in steadfast love to all who call upon you.

Colossians 1:13-14 He has delivered us from the domain of darkness and transferred us to the kingdom of his beloved Son, in whom we have redemption, the forgiveness of sins.

Matthew 6:14 For if you forgive others their trespasses, your heavenly Father will also forgive you...

Quotation

"Forgiving and being forgiven are two names for the same thing. The important thing is that a discord has been resolved." *C.S. Lewis*

Questions

- Do you find it hard to offer forgiveness to others?
- How do you feel when someone forgives you?
- Do you think forgiveness is a process?

May God Bless Your Week!!

© 2015 National Association of Christian Women Entrepreneurs * All Rights Reserved * www.nacwe.org

NACWE Word of the Week: Study and Discussion
September 7, 2015

The Word of the Week is PROSPER

Definition-PROSPER

verb
1. succeed in material terms; be financially successful.
2. flourish physically; grow strong and healthy.

synonyms: flourish, thrive, do well, bloom, blossom, burgeon, progress, do all right for oneself, get ahead, get on (in the world), be successful

Scripture

Jeremiah 29:11 NIV " For I know the plans I have for you," declares the LORD, "plans to prosper you and not to harm you, plans to give you hope and a future."

1 Kings 2:3 NIV "and observe what the LORD your God requires: Walk in obedience to him, and keep his decrees and commands, his laws and regulations, as written in the Law of Moses. Do this so that you may prosper in all you do and wherever you go"

Genesis 32:12 NIV "But you have said, 'I will surely make you prosper and will make your descendants like the sand of the sea, which cannot be counted.'"

Quotation

"The beginning of success starts first from strongly believing that God brought you into this life to prosper." *Edmond Mbiaka*

Questions

- What is your personal definition of prosperity?
- How do you plan to achieve it?

May God Bless Your Week!!

© 2015 National Association of Christian Women Entrepreneurs * All Rights Reserved * www.nacwe.org

NACWE Word of the Week: Study and Discussion
September 14, 2015

The Word of the Week is OBEDIENCE

Definition-OBEDIENCE

noun
1. an act or instance of obeying
2. the quality or state of being obedient

synonyms: Compliance, conformity, submission, subordination
antonyms: contrariness, rebellion, self-will, defiance, waywardness, noncompliance

Scripture

1 Samuel 15:22 (NLT) But Samuel replied, "What is more pleasing to the Lord: your burnt offerings and sacrifices or your obedience to his voice? Listen! Obedience is better than sacrifice, and submission is better than offering the fat of rams.

Deuteronomy 5:33 (NIV) Walk in obedience to all that the Lord your God has commanded you, so that you may live and prosper and prolong your days in the land that you will possess.

Romans 5:19 (NIV) For just as through the disobedience of the one man the many were made sinners, so also through the obedience of the one man the many will be made righteous.

2 John 1:6 (NIV) And this is love: that we walk in obedience to his commands. As you have heard from the beginning, his command is that you walk in love.

Quotation

"Obedience is the fruit of faith." – Christina Rossetti

Questions

- Does obedience have any 'gray' areas or it is clearly 'black or white'?
- Are there areas in your life where you struggle with obedience?

May God Bless Your Week!!

© 2015 National Association of Christian Women Entrepreneurs * All Rights Reserved * www.nacwe.org

NACWE Word of the Week: Study and Discussion
September 21, 2015

The Word of the Week is RESTORE

Definition-RESTORE

verb
1. bring back (a previous right, practice, custom, or situation); reinstate.
synonyms: reinstate, bring back, reinstitute, reimpose, reinstall, reestablish
2. return (someone or something) to a former condition, place, or position.
3. repair or renovate (a building, work of art, vehicle, etc.) so as to return it to its original condition.
synonyms: repair, fix, mend, refurbish, recondition, rehabilitate, rebuild, reconstruct, remodel, overhaul, redevelop, renovate

Scripture

Psalm 147:3 NASB He heals the brokenhearted and binds up their wounds.

Psalm 23:3 NASB He restores my soul; He guides me in the paths of righteousness for His name's sake.

2 Corinthians 13:11 ESV Finally, brothers, rejoice. Aim for restoration, comfort one another, agree with one another, live in peace; and the God of love and peace will be with you.

1 Peter 5:10 ESV And after you have suffered a little while, the God of all grace, who has called you to his eternal glory in Christ, will himself restore, confirm, strengthen, and establish you.

Quotation

"God restores. Completely. That's our Blessed assurance." *Andrena Sawyer*

Question

- How has God restored you?

© 2015 National Association of Christian Women Entrepreneurs * All Rights Reserved * www.nacwe.org

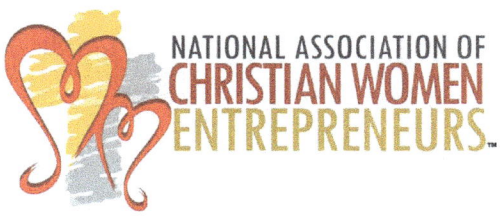

NACWE Word of the Week: Study and Discussion
September 28, 2015

The Word of the Week is PEACE

Definition-PEACE

Noun

1. Freedom from disturbance; quiet and tranquility.

synonyms: tranquility, calm, restfulness, peace and quiet, peacefulness, quiet, quietness

2. Freedom from or the cessation of war or violence.

synonyms: law and order, lawfulness, order, peacefulness, peaceableness, harmony, nonviolence; *formal* concord

Scripture

Isaiah 26:3 "You will keep him in perfect peace, whose mind is stayed on you, because he trusts in you."

John 14:27 "Peace I leave with you, My peace I give to you; not as the world gives do I give to you. Let not your heart be troubled, neither let it be afraid."

Philippians 4:6-7 "Be anxious for nothing, but in everything by prayer and supplication, with thanksgiving, let your requests be made known to God; and the peace of God, which surpasses all understanding, will guard your hearts and minds through Christ Jesus."

Quotation

"Peace cannot be kept by force; it can only be achieved by understanding." *Albert Einstein*

Question

- Do you struggle to have peace in your life?
- How or where do you find peace?

Praying God's peace in all of our lives. Have a blessed week.

© 2015 National Association of Christian Women Entrepreneurs * All Rights Reserved * www.nacwe.org

NACWE Word of the Week: Study and Discussion
October 5, 2015

The Word of the Week is COMFORT

Definition-COMFORT

noun
1. a state of physical ease and freedom from pain or constraint
2. the easing or alleviation of a person's feelings of grief or distress

synonyms: consolation, solace, condolence, sympathy, commiseration

Scripture

Psalm 23:4 (ESV) Even though I walk through the valley of the shadow of death, I will fear no evil, for you are with me; your rod and your staff, they comfort me.

Matthew 5:4 (NIV) Blessed are those who mourn, for they will be comforted.

2 Corinthians 1:3-4 (NIV) Praise be to the God and Father of our Lord Jesus Christ, the Father of compassion and the God of all comfort, who comforts us in all our troubles, so that we can comfort those in any trouble with the comfort we ourselves have received from God.

Philippians 2:1-2 (ESV) So if there is any encouragement in Christ, any comfort from love, any participation in the Spirit, any affection and sympathy, complete my joy by being of the same mind, having the same love, being in full accord (in one spirit) and of one mind.

Quotation

"The ultimate measure of a man is not where he stands in moments of comfort and convenience, but where he stands at times of challenge and controversy." – Martin Luther King, Jr.

Questions

- Is it more challenging for you to be "comforted" or to offer "comfort"?
- How does "comfort" play a role in your business?

May You receive His comfort with joy. May God Bless Your Week!!

© 2015 National Association of Christian Women Entrepreneurs * All Rights Reserved * www.nacwe.org

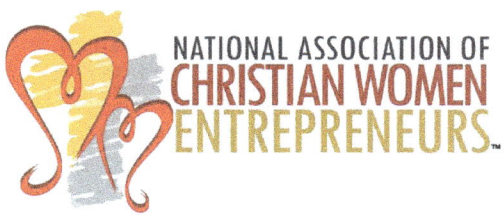

NACWE Word of the Week: Study and Discussion
October 12, 2015

The Word of the Week is Righteousness

Definition-Righteousness

noun
1. the quality of being morally right or justifiable

    Synonyms:
    all right, decent, ethical, honest, honorable, just, moral, nice, right, good, right-minded, straight, true, upright, virtuous

Scripture

Psalm 106:3 ESV Blessed are they who observe justice, who do righteousness at all times!

Isaiah 32:16-18 ESV Then justice will dwell in the wilderness, and righteousness abide in the fruitful field. And the effect of righteousness will be peace, and the result of righteousness, quietness and trust forever. My people will abide in a peaceful habitation, in secure dwellings, and in quiet resting places.

Romans 3:20 NIV "Therefore no one will be declared righteous in God's sight by the works of the law; rather, through the law we become conscious of our sin."

2 Timothy 2:22 ESV So flee youthful passions and pursue righteousness, faith, love, and peace, along with those who call on the Lord from a pure heart.

Quotation

"My righteousness is just as good as Jesus' righteousness, because it IS Jesus' righteousness!" — *E.W. Kenyon*

Questions

- Do you think of yourself as "righteous"?
- How do you explain righteousness to a non-believer?

May God Bless Your Week!!

© 2015 National Association of Christian Women Entrepreneurs * All Rights Reserved * www.nacwe.org

NACWE Word of the Week: Study and Discussion
October 19, 2015

The Word of the Week is TRUTH

Definition-Truth

noun
1. the quality or state of being true.

synonyms: veracity, truthfulness, verity, sincerity, candor, honesty; accuracy, correctness, validity, factuality, authenticity

2. that which is true or in accordance with fact or reality.
3. a fact or belief that is accepted as true.

Scripture

Psalm 15:1-2 O LORD, who shall sojourn in your tent? Who shall dwell on your holy hill? He who walks blamelessly and does what is right and speaks truth in his heart;

John 1:17 For the law was given through Moses; grace and truth came through Jesus Christ.

John 8:31-32 … So Jesus said to the Jews who had believed in him, "If you abide in my word, you are truly my disciples, and you will know the truth, and the truth will set you free."

Ephesians 1:13-14 In him you also, when you heard the word of truth, the gospel of your salvation, and believed in him, were sealed with the promised Holy Spirit, who is the guarantee of our inheritance until we acquire possession of it, to the praise of his glory.

Quotation
"Let us rejoice in the truth, wherever we find its lamp burning." ~ **Albert Schweitzer**

Questions
- Are you truthful?
- How do you feel when a person is not truthful with you?

I hope your week is productive and blessed.

© 2015 National Association of Christian Women Entrepreneurs * All Rights Reserved * www.nacwe.org

NACWE Word of the Week: Study and Discussion
October 29. 2015

The Word of the Week is: Stronghold

Definition- Stronghold
/strôNG hōld/noun

1. a place that has been fortified so as to protect it against attack.

synonyms: fortress, fort, castle, citadel, garrison

"the enemy stronghold"

2. a place where a particular cause or belief is strongly defended or upheld.
"a Republican stronghold"

synonyms: bastion, center, hotbed, safe seat

"a liberal stronghold"

Scripture

2 Samuel 22:3 The God of my strength, in whom I will trust; My shield and the horn of my salvation, My **stronghold** and my refuge; My Savior, You save me from violence. (NKJ)

Psalm 18:2 The LORD is my rock and my fortress and my deliverer; My God, my strength, in whom I will trust; My shield and the horn of my salvation, my **stronghold**. (NKJ)

Nahum 1:7 The LORD is good, A **stronghold** in the day of trouble; And He knows those who trust in Him. (NKJ)

Proverbs 10:29 The way of the LORD is a **stronghold** to those with integrity, but it destroys the wicked. (NLT)

Quotation

"Where does your security lie? Is God your refuge, your hiding place, your **stronghold**, your shepherd, your counselor, your friend, your redeemer, your savior, your guide? If He is, you don't need to search any further for security." ~ Elisabeth Elliot

"When I was about five, I gave my heart to Jesus Christ, and since then it's just been a **stronghold** in my life. Really, through the shark attack and all the hard times that my family and I went through, it gave us unity and perseverance to push through all this crazy stuff that we never knew was going to happen."
~ Bethany Hamilton

Questions

- Do you see Jesus as your stronghold?
- How do you feel knowing Jesus is your fortress, protector, stronghold?

© 2015 National Association of Christian Women Entrepreneurs * All Rights Reserved * www.nacwe.org

NACWE Word of the Week: Study and Discussion
November 2, 2015

The Word of the Week is PRAISE

Definition-PRAISE

verb

1. to say or write good things about (someone or something) : to express approval of (someone or something)

2. to express thanks to or love and respect for (God)

Scripture

Psalm 103:1-2 (NLT) Let all that I am praise the LORD; with my whole heart, I will praise his holy name. Let all that I am praise the LORD; may I never forget the good things he does for me.

Psalm 63:3 (NASB) Because Your lovingkindness is better than life, my lips will praise You.

Acts 16:25-26 (NASB) But about midnight Paul and Silas were praying and singing hymns of praise to God, and the prisoners were listening to them; and suddenly there came a great earthquake, so that the foundations of the prison house were shaken; and immediately all the doors were opened and everyone's chains were unfastened.

James 5:13 (NASB) Is anyone among you suffering? Then he must pray. Is anyone cheerful? He is to sing praises.

Quotation

"God lives in the place of praise. If we want to be where He is, we need to go to His address." – Nancy Leigh DeMoss

Questions

- Do you find it challenging to praise God no matter your circumstances?
- What role does praise play in your life/business?

© 2015 National Association of Christian Women Entrepreneurs * All Rights Reserved * www.nacwe.org

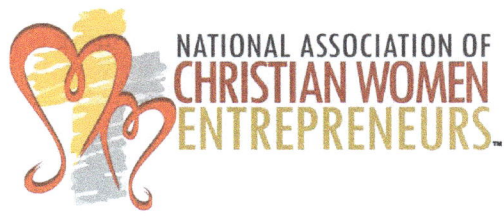

NACWE Word of the Week: Study and Discussion
November 9, 2015

The Word of the Week is FELLOWSHIP

Definition-FELLOWSHIP

Noun
- friendly association, especially with people who share one's interests.

synonyms: companionship, companionability, sociability, comradeship, camaraderie, friendship, mutual support; togetherness, solidarity

Scripture

Psalm 55:14 NASB We who had sweet fellowship together walked in the house of God in the throng.

Acts 2:42 NIV They devoted themselves to the apostles' teaching and to fellowship, to the breaking of bread and to prayer.

1 John 1:7 NIV But if we walk in the light, as he is in the light, we have fellowship with one another, and the blood of Jesus, his Son, purifies us from all sin.

2 Corinthians 13:14 NIV May the grace of the Lord Jesus Christ, and the love of God, and the fellowship of the Holy Spirit be with you all.

Quotation

"I want the whole Christ for my Savior, the whole Bible for my book, the whole Church for my fellowship, and the whole world for my mission field." ~ *John Wesley*

Questions

- Do you fellowship with other believers?
- How important is it to you?

Blessings on your week.

© 2015 National Association of Christian Women Entrepreneurs * All Rights Reserved * www.nacwe.org

NACWE Word of the Week: Study and Discussion
November 16, 2015

The Word of the Week is THANKSGIVING

Definition-THANKSGIVING

noun
1. the expression of gratitude, especially to God.
2. (in North America) an annual national holiday marked by religious observances and a traditional meal including turkey. The holiday commemorates a harvest festival celebrated by the Pilgrims in 1621, and is held in the US on the fourth Thursday in November. A similar holiday is held in Canada, usually on the second Monday in October.

Scripture

Jeremiah 33:11 (NIV) the sounds of joy and gladness, the voices of bride and bridegroom, and the voices of those who bring thank offerings to the house of the LORD, saying, "Give thanks to the LORD Almighty, for the LORD is good; his love endures forever." For I will restore the fortunes of the land as they were before,' says the LORD.

Psalm 100:4 (NIV) Enter his gates with thanksgiving and his courts with praise; give thanks to him and praise his name.

Corinthians 1:4 (NIV) I always thank God for you because of his grace given you in Christ Jesus.

2 Corinthians 4:15-16 (NIV) All this is for your benefit, so that the grace that is reaching more and more people may cause thanksgiving to overflow to the glory of God. Therefore we do not lose heart. Though outwardly we are wasting away, yet inwardly we are being renewed day by day.

Quotation

"Thanksgiving Day is a jewel, to set in the hearts of honest men; but be careful that you do not take the day, and leave out the gratitude." *E.P. Powell*

Questions

- Who and What are you thankful for?

© 2015 National Association of Christian Women Entrepreneurs * All Rights Reserved * www.nacwe.org

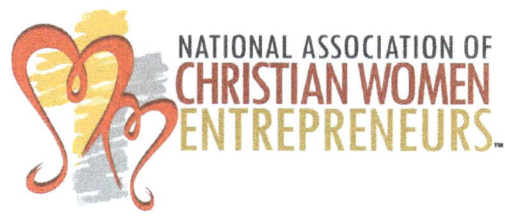

NACWE Word of the Week: Study and Discussion
November 30, 2015

The Word of the Week is PURPOSE

Definition-PURPOSE

Noun
1. the reason for which something is done or created or for which something exists.
synonyms: motive, motivation, grounds, cause, occasion, reason, point, basis, justification intention, aim, object, objective, goal, end, plan, scheme, target; ambition, aspiration

Scripture

Exodus 9:16 (NIV) But I have raised you up for this very purpose, that I might show you my power and that my name might be proclaimed in all the earth.

Proverbs 19:21 (NIV) Many are the plans in a person's heart, but it is the Lord's purpose that prevails.

Romans 8:28 (NIV) And we know that in all things God works for the good of those who love him, who have been called according to his purpose.

2 Timothy 1:9 (NIV) He has saved us and called us to a holy life—not because of anything we have done but because of his own purpose and grace.

Quotation

"Without God, life has no purpose, and without purpose, life has no meaning. Without meaning, life has no significance or hope." - *Rick Warren*

Questions

- Do you know your purpose in life?
- How do you fulfill your purpose? In your personal life? In your career?

May God bless you in all of these areas of your life.

© 2015 National Association of Christian Women Entrepreneurs * All Rights Reserved * www.nacwe.org

NACWE Word of the Week: Study and Discussion
December 7, 2015

The Word of the Week is INSPIRE

Definition-INSPIRE

Verb
1. fill (someone) with the urge or ability to do or feel something, especially to do something creative.

synonyms: stimulate, motivate, encourage, influence, rouse, move, stir, energize, galvanize, incite; animate, fire, excite, spark, inspirit, incentivize, affect, inspirational, encouraging, heartening, uplifting, stirring, rousing, stimulating, electrifying; moving, affecting, impassioned, influential

Scripture

Timothy 3:16-17 (HCSB) All Scripture is inspired by God and is profitable for teaching, for rebuking, for correcting, for training in righteousness, so that the man of God may be complete, equipped for every good work.

Isaiah 40:28-31 (NIV) Do you not know? Have you not heard? The LORD is the everlasting God, the Creator of the ends of the earth. He will not grow tired or weary, and his understanding no one can fathom. He gives strength to the weary and increases the power of the weak. Even youths grow tired and weary, and young men stumble and fall; but those who hope in the LORD will renew their strength. They will soar on wings like eagles; they will run and not grow weary, they will walk and not be faint.

Quotation

"If your actions inspire others to dream more, learn more, do more and become more, you are a leader." *John Quincy Adams*

Questions

- Who or what INSPIRERS you?
- How do you INSPIRE others?

Praying God's blessing on you and your business.

© 2015 National Association of Christian Women Entrepreneurs * All Rights Reserved * www.nacwe.org

NACWE Word of the Week: Study and Discussion
December 14, 2015

The Word of the Week is CELEBRATE

Definition- CELEBRATE

Verb

- publicly acknowledge (a significant or happy day or event) with a social gathering or enjoyable activity.

synonyms: commemorate, observe, mark, keep, honor, remember, memorialize

Scripture

1 Corinthians 5:8 (ESV) Let us therefore celebrate the festival, not with the old leaven, the leaven of malice and evil, but with the unleavened bread of sincerity and truth.

Ecclesiastes 3:13 (ESV) Also that everyone should eat and drink and take pleasure in all his toil—this is God's gift to man.

Ecclesiastes 3:4 (ESV) A time to weep, and a time to laugh; a time to mourn, and a time to dance

Matthew 2:11 (ESV) And going into the house they saw the child with Mary his mother, and they fell down and worshiped him. Then, opening their treasures, they offered him gifts, gold and frankincense and myrrh.

Quotation

"The more you praise and celebrate your life, the more there is in life to celebrate."
― Oprah Winfrey

Questions

- How do you celebrate life?
- Do you need to celebrate more?

Praying God's blessing on you and your business.

© 2015 National Association of Christian Women Entrepreneurs * All Rights Reserved * www.nacwe.org